Praise for *Acting*

"A good beginning step for anyone who wants to understand the industry in Los Angeles."
— Efren Ramirez, Actor
(*Napoleon Dynamite, Employee of the Month, Crank*)

"I can't thank Christian Campos enough for updating and creating this breakdown to help guide new, upcoming actors who feel lost and don't know where to start. *Acting Today* just made your life easier. This is exactly how I got started. You can only know so many people who have experienced all sides in the field and truly know what they are talking about. If you want to get started the right way, this book is for you."
— Lisseth Chavez, Actress (*The Fosters, Greys Anatomy, The OA*)

"Christian Campos speaks from a place of grounded pragmatism and provides the groundwork for an effective break into the Los Angeles entertainment industry—he's done the hard work for you."
—Benjamin W. Decker, Author
(*Practical Meditation for Beginners*)

"I met Christian Campos on the set of *90210* years ago, when I first started. He immediately reached out to me and helped me learn the ways on set. Christian was always one to share his knowledge. One thing we had in common was our passion for film. I remember Christian was working on an audition—actually, every time I saw Christian he was working on an audition. Christian has been a student of the game and over the years he truly has mastered what it takes to make a living out of his passion. I followed Christian's career and watched him book job after job. If you are serious about being an actor, read this book. *Acting Today* will help make your dream a reality."
—Nayip Ramos, Director (*Disney Channel, ABC*)

"I've been a working actor in Hollywood for 40 years. I'm frequently asked, 'How do I get into show business?' This comprehensive guide will answer ALL your questions! I've known Christian Campos since he was a little boy. I've watched him grow and pursue his dream to be a successful actor. Now he's written this book to help others pursue theirs."

—Sloan Robinson, Actress
(*Lucifer, The Neighborhood, Two Broke Girls*)

"When an individual feels that itch from within that says, 'I want to be an actor,' immediately the first thing needed is honest information that is trusted. Where and how does one get started? You've heard the saying, 'knowledge is power' so this book is a MUST."

—Bobby Gene, Acting Coach (*Bobby Gene's Actors Clubhouse*)

"It's hard to begin a career as an actor without a mentor or direction. *Acting Today* is like a new pair of glasses. It changes your view of the industry."

—Carlos Pratts, Actor (*McFarland USA, Paranormal Activity: The Marked Ones, The Bridge*)

"This book by far contains the best 'industry golden nuggets' I've yet to read. It stands as a strong, action driven guidance tool on how to build your business as an actor. Even 'advanced' actors can benefit from this incredible book. If you are serious about building your empire, then I highly recommend reading this book."

—Orel De La Mota, Actor (*Titans, NCIS LA, Grace & Frankie*)

ACTING TODAY

A Guide to Hollywood's New Era

CHRISTIAN CAMPOS

BOOKED IT
PRESS

ISBN: 978-0-578-54077-1 (Print Edition)
ISBN: 978-0-578-55193-7 (eBook Edition)

Booked It Press
www.bookeditpress.com

Cover Design: Lee Cyril Singkala / Broken Anchor Digital
https://brokenanchordigital.com

Editing & Book Design: Integrative Ink
www.integrativeink.com

Library of Congress Control Number: 2019910215

CONTENTS

FOREWORD

When I first started my acting career in the early '90s, I had no guide, mentor, or any way of knowing the steps to follow in order to begin working in the entertainment industry. Back then, I had to learn everything about show business through experience. Email, social media, and digital platforms for actors did not exist, so I would literally go knocking on the doors of talent agencies and casting offices for networking-employment opportunities. Fair to say, it was an active approach and hustle during that time in Hollywood, more so than today.

On that note, if you're an aspiring actor right now and you're searching for early career guidance and effective knowledge in show business, then I would like to ask you this question: "Do you want to be a working actor?" If your answer is yes, then I would highly recommend getting this book and following all the steps. Honestly, if I had this book when I started acting, then everything would have been so much easier because I would have been so much more prepared. With that in mind, many thanks to Christian Campos for writing such an amazing, insightful, and incredibly helpful book for all the aspiring actors out there. If you want to be a professional actor, then *Acting Today* is definitely the book for you to start your career. REAL TALK.

Noel Gugliemi
(a.k.a. Noel G, Hector)

INTRODUCTION

Like many of you, when I was young, I dreamed about acting watching Disney movies and TV shows. Both of my parents migrated from Guatemala in the '80s to pursue a better life. My older brother, Pierre, and I are first generation-born American citizens. My parents did not know English yet, so naturally when I was born in 1987, they only spoke to me in Spanish.

When I began elementary school at the age of five, I immediately struggled in school since everything was in English. With the help of my school teachers, I quickly learned the language. I am eternally grateful to my parents for having taught me Spanish as my first language. Today, I am bilingual, and I have booked many national commercials in both markets.

It wasn't in deck of cards to become an actor. My parents didn't have a television growing up in Guatemala, and there's no history of having had family members who were performers.

My journey as an actor began in the year 2003, at the age of fifteen. I was attending Manual Arts High School in South Central Los Angeles, where my acting coach, Bobby

Gene, stopped by to do an outstanding acting showcase in our auditorium. After the showcase ended, Bobby extended an invitation to all students to audition that Saturday for a free three-month scholarship at his Actors Club House. I was blown away by the opportunity that had presented itself. This was my shot to start acting.

That Saturday, I went to audition at the clubhouse and became aware that he was only selecting ten actors for the free scholarship. We were handed commercial scripts to choose from and, believe it or not, after everyone performed, I was the tenth kid to get picked.

At the Bobby Gene's Actors Club House, I began my journey in acting and learned Scene Study, On-Camera Commercial Acting, and Improvisation. I was fortunate enough to have learned these techniques from my instructors Efren Ramirez (*Napoleon Dynamite, Crank, Employee of the Month*) and Bob Bancroft (*Zenon: Girl of the 21ˢᵗ Century, Very Bad Things, The Wedding Pact*).

My first commercial audition—given to me by my instructor, Bobby—I ended up booking. I remember receiving a copy of it on VHS Tape. I remember my first headshot being printed in Black and White, since they were popular back then.

Today, I have been in hit shows such as *Criminal Minds*, *NCIS*, *East Los High*, and have continued to book many national commercials for worldwide companies, such as Pepsi, AT&T, Best Buy, and Adidas. For years now, I've received multiples messages from friends and strangers seeking advice on how to start acting, which inspired me to write this book. Throughout my career, I've done it all: Background Acting, Stand-in, Inserts, Photo Double, Stunts, Voiceover, Modeling, and Principal Acting. In my seventeen years in the field of Acting, I've met some of the most magnificent actors, most of whom made the big move to Los Angeles.

Not having any direction on how to begin your acting career can be very scary. Bobby Gene changed my life by jumpstarting my acting career. My intention is to pay it forward and give you a direction to jumpstart your new acting career.

TV, commercials, and films have evolved throughout the years. It's a process to learn all the knowledge, wisdom, secrets, and tips in Hollywood. My entire heart is in this book to make it easier for you and to give you the strength to take that big step and change your life forever. This is The New Era of Acting.

NEW TO LA

L os Angeles, California is the heart and center of film-
making. This is where it's happening, this is where it's
at, and this is where you need to be. Moving to Los Angeles can be a big first step. It can be scary—especially if you
aren't familiar with this city. If you are considering making
the big move out here, I can assure you it won't be easy. It's
difficult being away from your friends and family, but you
will be one step closer to your dream. You are a dreamer,
and that's what makes you special. People like you truly

change the world. You are a performer, a person who entertains an audience. You are a risk-taker, and with your ambition, drive, and determination, you will succeed. You cannot fail if you never give up. I believe in you.

A lot of talent who move to Los Angeles to pursue Acting and Modeling may find themselves easily distracted because of the lifestyle here. There's a lot going on and a lot to do every day—from night clubs and cool bars to celebrity parties and big events. I urge you not to get distracted by these things. Stay on your path and settle in your first year.

It's imperative that you move out here with a plan. If you are an independent person, living in Los Angeles can be expensive. My advice is to reach out to friends and family already living here for housing recommendations. If you have neither of these, seeking a roommate is a good idea. Nowadays, we have the Internet and apps where you can find a roommate. Airbnb and Craigslist are great for finding your new home in Los Angeles.

There are a wide variety of neighborhoods in Los Angeles, but I recommend you find a place that isn't too far from Hollywood, since that's where the majority of your auditions will take place. Many actors move to Studio City and North Hollywood. These are great locations and close to Hollywood, but they can be a bit pricey. Many dancers, models, and actors live in these locations.

Studio City is home to CBS Studios. It's got hiking trails, sushi houses, and stylish gastro pubs.

North Hollywood is down the street from Universal Studios Hollywood. You can take a nice walk to North Hollywood's Arts district, which offers art galleries, dance studios, and great restaurants. If you decide to live in **Hollywood**, keep in mind that there's a lot going on. Hollywood hardly sleeps. It's very crowded, traffic is usually a nightmare, it's packed with tourists, and it can be very expensive. However, you'll be living where most of your auditions will take place.

West Hollywood is a great and safe location. It's known for its high-energy nightlife and is very popular with the Lesbian, Gay, Bisexual, Transgendered, and Queer (or questioning) community. It is also home to a number of gay bars, dance clubs, great restaurants, and shops.

Culver City is a nice, quiet place in which to live. Home to Sony Pictures Studios and Downtown Culver City, which also offers art galleries, fine dining, and night clubs.

Los Feliz is super relaxed. Its cafes and restaurants are amazing. The neighborhood borders Griffith Park, which is great for hiking and picnics on a beautiful day out in sunny California.

Not many people know about **Silver Lake**. This neighborhood fully embraces the hipster lifestyle. It is known for its cool street art, coffee shops, indie music venues, Asian eateries, trendy bars, and a beautiful dog park.

If you are looking for something more affordable, I personally recommend living in **Koreatown**. I was born and raised in Koreatown and lived there for twenty-nine years. Koreatown is known for its karaoke joints, speakeasies, spas, flashy clubs, and of course the best Korean BBQ. It can get crowded, and finding parking after 5:00 p.m. can be a nightmare. If you decide to move to Koreatown, I highly suggest you get an apartment that offers parking so you won't have to deal with this problem.

The great thing about living in Koreatown is that you are literally ten minutes away from Downtown Los Angeles. Downtown Los Angeles is my favorite place to be. Staples Center, LA Live, Microsoft Theatre, The Walt Disney Concert Hall, and our latest attraction, OUE Skyspace, are all located in Downtown Los Angeles.

Another great fact about living in Los Angeles is that you can get around the cities I mentioned within twenty-five minutes. Everything is close by—if you aren't driving during high traffic hours, of course. Keep in mind that during high traffic hours, you can be stuck driving for one hour, minimum. To my knowledge, being from here and living here my entire life, high traffic hours run from 7:00 a.m. to 9:30 a.m. and again from 3:00 p.m. to 7:30 p.m. Keep in mind that leaving ten minutes later than you originally planned can make a big difference. Always leave on time. If you do not drive, Lyft, Uber, and public transportation are always of great help.

The following is a list of cities in which you may want to consider living in order to be close to auditions:

Santa Monica, Beverly Hills, Pasadena, West Hollywood, Culver City, Venice, Torrance, Burbank, Woodland Hills, Canoga Park, Encino, Sherman Oaks, Studio City, Burbank, North Hollywood, Glendale, Marina Del Rey, Van Nuys, Reseda, Panorama City, Arleta, Sun Valley, Chatsworth, Northridge, Playa Vista, Carson, Playa Del Rey, Universal City, Century City, Baldwin Park, Westwood, Valley Village, Mission Hills, Downey, North Hills, Pacoima, Eagle Rock, and East LA.

GETTING AN AGENT

There are different approaches to signing with an agent. You want to avoid calling an agency or agent directly by phone. This action might irritate an agent and will definitely reflect badly on your end. If you search any acting agency on the web, they usually have submission instructions. You want to follow those steps and do exactly what they ask of you. Normally, they attach an email and have you send in your headshots, resume, contact information, and sizes.

Another approach would be finding a great acting school that brings in agents from time to time to scout and potentially sign new talent. This is called a showcase. Your acting coach will bring in theatrical and commercial agents to watch you showcase your acting skills. If an agent is interested in you, he will then proceed to give your acting coach their information, along with a location date and time for you to come in and audition for them, for possible representation.

Acting schools that offer showcases to agencies are the ones I recommend. Sometimes agents will search for new talent through actor's websites. That's how my agent found me years ago. I received a message from him through LA Casting asking me to come in and read for him for representation.

Lastly, you can mail in a solid cover letter, your head-shots, resume, and reel the old fashion way, with a big yellow envelope to their address and hope to hear back from them.

If you have zero work to show an agent, building an acting reel is encouraged. An acting reel is comprised of different short clips of yourself edited together, demonstrating your acting skills. A great acting reel can sign you with an agent. You want to keep your reel between 3–5 minutes. There's plenty of companies that can shoot you an acting reel, but they can be expensive. Film schools with students working on their Cycle Films and Final Thesis Films are a great way to build up your acting reel for free. Some film students actually pay *you* to work on their films. You can always physically drop off your headshot at a film school's front desk and hope to hear from a student.

Back in the day, it used to be very difficult to sign with an agent if you weren't a union actor. Now, there's a lot of non-union work out there, which makes it easier for an agent to consider and sign you. Having an agent is extremely important because they see 100% of the material that is out there. When you see actors on television shows and films, I can assure you they got their auditions through their agents. Getting an episodic or feature film audition by yourself is very difficult, since casting directors go the agent route because they know they can trust the already signed working actors.

A **Manager** usually works the same way an agent does. An agent takes 10% of your earnings, while a manager can take up to 15%. Getting a manager isn't a bad idea. Managers tend to have a smaller roster when it comes to their clients, so they focus more on you. Managers have more of a personal relationship with their clients and, like agents, they can also get you through the door when it comes to auditions. When it comes to looking for the right project for you or giving you their best advice, a manager is great to have.

Keep in mind that if you have both an agent and manager, that's 20% off your paycheck. However, if you have both, you'll have an entire team working for you in your career. You don't necessarily need a manager to be successful. I advise that you get a manager if you are already a working actor and have a lot on your plate.

Additional note: Managers aren't franchised by the Unions or licensed by the state. SAG-AFTRA'S website advises you to always have an attorney review your contract with a manager before signing.

The following is a list of 70 Talent Agencies in Los Angeles as of 2019

90210 TALENT AGENCY
www.90210talent.com

ABRAMS ARTISTS AGENCY
www.abramsartists.com

ACROSS THE BOARD TALENT AGENCY
www.atbtalent.com

AFFINITY ARTISTS AGENCY
www.affinityartists.com

AGENCY FOR THE PERFORMING ARTS (APA)
www.apa-agency.com

AKA TALENT AGENCY
www.akatalent.com

ALLEGORY CREATIVE TALENT
www.allegorytalent.com

ALMOND TALENT AGENCY
www.almondtalent.com

AMSEL EISENSTADT FRAZIER & HINOJOSA TALENT AGENCY (AEFH)
www.aeftalent.com

AQUA TALENT AGENCY
www.aquatalent.com

ARTISTIC TALENT
www.artistictalentla.com

ATLAS TALENT AGENCY
www.atlastalent.com

AVALON ARTISTS GROUP
www.avalonartists.com

BBA TALENT
www.bbatalent.com

BETH STEIN & ASSOCIATES
www.bethsteinandassociates.com

BLACK APPLE TALENT
www.blackappletalent.com

BRADY BRANNON & RICH TALENT (BBR)
www.bbrtalentagency.com

BRS/GAGE TALENT AGENCY
www.brsgage.com

BUCHWALD AGENCY
www.buchwald.com

CENTRAL ARTISTS
www.centralartists.com

CLEAR TALENT GROUP
www.cleartalentgroup.com

COAST TO COAST
www.ctctalent.com

CREATIVE ARTISTS AGENCY (CAA)
www.caa.com

CUNNINGHAM ESCOTT SLEVIN & DOHERTY (CESD)
www.cesdtalent.com

DANIEL HOFF AGENCY
www.danielhoffagency.com

DDO ARTISTS AGENCY
www.ddoagency.com

DEFINING ARTISTS AGENCY
www.definingartists.com

ELEMENT TALENT AGENCY
www.elementtalent.com

ELLIS TALENT GROUP
www.ellistalentgroup.com

ENGAGE ARTISTS AGENCY (EAA)
www.engageartists.com

ERIS TALENT AGENCY
www.eristalentagency.com

FIRESTARTER ENTERTAINMENT
www.firestarterentertainment.com

GLOBAL ARTISTS AGENCY
www.globalartistsagency.net

GREENE & ASSOCIATES TALENT AGENCY
www.greentalent.com

GVA TALENT AGENCY
www.gvatalent.com

HENDERSON REPRESENTS
www.hritalent.com

HERVEY/GRIMES TALENT AGENCY
www.herveygrimes.com

ICM PARTNERS
www.icmpartners.com

INNOVATIVE ARTISTS
www.innovativeartists.com

J PERVIS TALENT AGENCY
www.jpervistalent.com

JERRY PACE AGENCY
www.jerrypaceagency.com

KATHLEEN SCHULTZ ASSOCIATES TALENT AGENCY (KSA)
www.kathleenschultzassociates.com

KAZARIAN/MEASURES/RUSKIN & ASSOCIATES
www.kmrtalent.com

LA TALENT
www.latalent.com

LINDA MCALISTER TALENT
www.lmtalent.com

LITTMAN TALENT GROUP
www.littmantalent.com

MAVRICK ARTISTS AGENCY
www.mavrickartists.com

MEDIA ARTISTS GROUP
www.mediaartistsgroup.com

MICHAEL ZANUCK AGENCY (MZA)
www.mzaagency.com

MOGAN ENTERTAINMENT
www.moganentertainment.com

MOMENTUM TALENT AND LITERARY AGENCY
www.momentumtalent.com

OSBRINK TALENT AGENCY
www.osbrinkagency.com

PANTHEON TALENT
www.pantheontalent.com

PARADIGM TALENT AGENCY
www.paradigmagency.com

ROGERS ORION TALENT AGENCY
www.rogersorion.com

RPM TALENT AGENCY
www.rpmtalent.com

SAVAGE AGENCY
www.savageagency.net

SMS TALENT
www.smstalent.com

SOVEREIGN TALENT GROUP
www.sovereigntg.com

TALENT HOUSE LA
www.thetalenthousela.com

TALENTWORKS
www.talentworksla.com

TCA MGMT
www.tcamgmt.com

TCA/JED ROOT
www.tcajedroot.com

THE GERSH AGENCY
www.gershagency.com

THE JACKSON AGENCY
www.thejacksonagency.com

THE KOHNER AGENCY
www.paulkohner.com

THE POLYGON GROUP
www.thepolygongroup.com

THE WAYNE AGENCY
www.thewayneagency.com

UNITED TALENT AGENCY (UTA)
www.unitedtalent.com

WILLIAM MORRIS ENDEAVOR (WME)
www.wmeetertainment.com

PROVING YOURSELF TO YOUR AGENT

When you first sign with an agency, they will put you to the test by giving you a few auditions right away. If you don't book any of your auditions your first months, you may not hear from them for a while. This is exactly why you hear many actors complaining about their agents not sending them out much or working hard for them and eventually leave to seek different representation. You have to keep in mind that agencies have a lot of clients who are consistently booking, some of whom are series regulars on television shows. These clients who book and work regularly become your agent's priority, putting you at the bottom of their list.

When I first signed with my agent, I dealt with this problem but decided to take a different approach to the situation. Instead of seeking different representation, I decided to prove myself to my agent. I did this by not relying on him and, instead, booking projects myself. I submitted myself on actor's websites, such as LA Casting, Actors Access, and Casting Frontier, and I got myself plenty of auditions without my agent.

Every time I'd book a Commercial or Print job, I'd immediately call my agent to let him know about it, and of course cut him in on the profits. He was very happy. I wanted him to know that I was working my ass off and not relying on him, but most importantly, that I kept him in mind. I then realized that by doing this action, my agent began to give me more auditions and noticed me more.

Always keep in mind that it's a team effort between you and your agent. You can't be greedy or have that mindset. It should be 50/50 on both sides. You should both be working equally as hard for each other. You want to maintain a great relationship with your agent to succeed in this game. Relationships aren't easy. You need to communicate well, respect each other, trust each other, and most importantly, believe in each other. That's the kind of relationship you should strive for with your agent in order to be successful.

Don't be like many actors here in Hollywood who sit around and wait for their agents to call them and give them auditions. As a struggling actor, you are in survival mode, and you have to keep that mentality. You have to learn to be a hustler, a go-getter. This is why I look up to actors like Dwayne Johnson, Kevin Hart, and Mark Wahlberg. Even though they've already made it, they don't hold that mindset. They're up at 5:00 a.m. or earlier almost every day. They work super hard, kick the day in the ass, and always strive for more.

ACTOR'S WEBSITES

When you first sign with an agent, you are immediately instructed to join the following actor's websites: **Actors Access, LA Casting,** and **Casting Frontier**. Agents use these websites to receive casting alerts and send out your profile and resume to casting directors to get you auditions. Through these websites, agents are able to view numerous casting breakdowns for Films, Short Films, Commercials, Music Videos, and Print jobs that may be the right fit for you. If there's a casting that fits your description, your agent will then proceed to submit your profile in order to get you an audition.

You do not necessarily need to be signed with an agency to join these actor's websites. These websites charge you an affordable monthly fee or a one-time yearly fee to access them. Once you are signed up with these websites, you can then set up your profile with Headshots, Sizes, Resume, and personal information. You are also able to self-submit to extra and principal paid projects. If you already have an agent and list them under you in these websites, you'll get a monthly discount.

Many actors underestimate these websites. I myself have booked many acting jobs, including national commercials, without my agent by self-submitting. As I've mentioned previously, do not sit around on your ass and wait on your agent to get you auditions. When using these websites, your email will become your life. You will begin to receive casting notifications through your email regarding projects that fit your description. These websites normally have a section in them where they ask whether you'd like to receive notifications for castings. Make sure you check that box, or you will miss out on these casting notifications.

There are thousands of actors who use these websites and receive casting notifications daily, so keep in mind that if you do not submit your profile within the first ten minutes of the posting, you will not get the audition.

If you are a big social media user and check your phone constantly, I suggest you apply that same amount of energy to checking your email. You do not want to miss out on a casting notice because you were too busy checking out a friend's post on Instagram. Remember, this is your career, and you are here now, so make it happen. Uploading the right photos to these websites can make the biggest difference in the world. Aside from your common theatrical and commercial Headshots, you will want to upload photos in uniform as well.

Examples: *Soccer look, Nurse look, Fitness look,* even a *Couple photo,* if you have a significant other. Having these looks uploaded on ACTOR'S WEBSITES give you an advantage over thousands of actors. When you submit for a project, the casting director will immediately see what you look like "in uniform" and bring you in to audition.

Soccer Look

Nurse Look

Couple

INVESTING IN YOUR CAREER

HEADSHOTS

A good headshot can get you in the room. Spending a couple hundred dollars on a good photographer is worth the investment in the long run. Think of it this way: you spend $300 with a photographer to take your new headshot. That headshot gets you an audition, and you end up booking the commercial. The commercial pays $3,000. You see what I mean? Definitely worth the investment. You have to invest in your career to get results. I wouldn't worry too much about paying to print out headshots. Many casting directors no longer request them, since your profile and information are already online. Everything is completed electronically.

Commercial Headshots are fun and playful. They are intended only to be used in the commercial world and in print. The focus is on your smile. Open mouth smile, closed-lip smile, or a smirk are always great. Wearing soft colors is a great choice.

Examples: *Royal Blue, Teal, Burgundy, Yellow, Lavender, Baby Blue, Pink, and Red.*

You want to stay away from black and white. Layers are a great choice and can be darker: Jackets, Hoodies, and Flannels.

Theatrical Headshots are only to be used in Television and Films. These headshots are more intense and serious. You have to be able to tell a story with your look. Darker colors are a great choice.

Examples: *Black, Gray, Brown, Beige, Dark Green, Red, Burgundy, and Dark Blue.*

Layers are also a great choice: Long Sleeve Denims, Jackets, Hoodies, and Flannels.

WARDROBE / COSTUMES

As an actor, you get to play anything you can possibly think of: Doctor, Nurse, Soldier, Fireman, etc. I strongly recommend investing in different types of costumes, which you think will come in handy down the line. I own all sports attire, military attire, plain red and blue polo shirts for commercial auditions, and medical scrubs. Shopping at thrift shops is very affordable and reliable. There are plenty of Goodwill thrift shops that own these costumes in this city. Keep in mind that you always want to go in costume to your auditions. Not many actors do, and that will give you an advantage to get the callback or even book it.

RINGLIGHT

Acting has changed throughout the years. A lot of directors, producers, and casting directors do not have time to have you physically come in to audition; instead, they'll have you send in a self-tape. A self-tape is a video audition you shoot yourself in your own home—usually with a  plain white background. Not many actors own a Ring Light, or know how useful they can be. Ring Lights are perfect for self-taping. A Ring Light is a lighting tool shaped like a ring and comes with a stand. It is mainly used by makeup artists but is perfect for actors. You can purchase a Ring Light online or in any electronics store. If you are on a budget and want to save yourself a couple of bucks, I recommend looking for one on any of these apps: Offer Up, Letgo, or 5 Miles. People sell new or used ones on these apps, and if you are lucky enough, as I was, you may find one at a very affordable price.

UNION VS. NON-UNION

When you are starting out in your career as an actor, you are considered to be a Non-Union performer. A Non-Union performer is an actor who has not yet joined the union SAG-AFTRA. The difference between a NON-UNION performer and a UNION performer is that, when booking a Commercial or Television job that's considered to be Non-Union, you won't get any residuals/royalties from it. However, if you get the opportunity to audition and book a National Commercial or Television Guest Star on a UNION project, you can make thousands of dollars in residuals. Every time the project you were in airs on television, you'll get a percentage from it. You can easily make over $10,000 booking a UNION National Commercial today, since you get Internet, Cable, Television, and even Social Media checks.

If you are serious in succeeding in your career as an actor/actress, you must aim to join SAG-AFTRA. As a SAG-AFTRA member, you also get benefits, such as discounts at restaurants, makeup accessories, free entry to certain theatres, and movie screeners at the end of the year for voting purposes. SAG-AFTRA will always be there to protect you and answer any questions you have regarding a problem on-set or any other issues. You are also able to track down your residuals on their website or change your address in case you move. SAG-AFTRA always sends out representatives to sets spontaneously to make sure Union members are taken care of with food, water, and safety.

You need to have worked three UNION background jobs to get invited to join the SAG-AFTRA. These Union background jobs do not come around easy if you are Non-Union. Another way to become a SAG-AFTRA member is to audition and book a Union project as a principal performer. If that were to occur, production will have no other alternative than to **Taft-Hartley** you. Getting Taft-Hartley is the best thing that can happen to you. It is your golden ticket to Willy Wonka's Chocolate Factory. Being Taft-Hartley means you will no longer need three Union vouchers to be eligible to join SAG-AFTRA—you will automatically be eligible to join right away.

Today, it costs $3,000 to join SAG-AFTRA, according to their website. You can save some money and pay up front or get a loan through SAG-AFTRA and set up a payment plan. There are several SAG-AFTRA offices spread throughout the United States, in case you ever have any additional questions. If you want to elevate yourself to the next level of success, I strongly encourage you to pursue a career as a SAG-AFTRA performer. SAG-AFTRA jobs are where you'll always be protected and taken care of financially as a professional actor.

The following is a list of SAG-AFTRA offices throughout the country as of 2019

NATIONAL HEADQUARTERS
5757 Wilshire Blvd.
Los Angeles, CA 90036
(855) 724-2387
info@sagaftra.org

NEW YORK
1900 Broadway, 5th Floor
New York, New York 10023
(212) 944-1030
newyork@sag-aftra.org

ATLANTA
3565 Piedmont Rd. NE, Piedmont
Center, Bldg. 2, Suite 720
Atlanta, GA 30305
(404) 239-0131
atlanta@sagaftra.org

CHICAGO
1 East Erie, Suite #650
Chicago, Illinois 60611
(312) 573-8081
chicago@sagaftra.org

DALLAS-FORT WORTH
15110 Dallas Parkway, Suite 440
Dallas, Texas 75248
(214) 363-8300
dallas@sagaftra.org

HAWAII
201 Merchant St., Suite 2301
Honolulu, Hawaii 96813-2929
(808) 596-0388
hawaii@sagaftra.org

MIAMI
3470 N.W. 82nd Avenue, Suite 780
Doral, Florida 33122-1024
(305) 670-7677
miami@sagaftra.org

MISSOURI VALLEY
1034 South Brentwood Blvd, Suite 1310
St. Louis, Missouri 63117
(314) 231-8410

NASHVILLE
1108 17th Ave. South
Nashville, Tennessee 37212
(615) 327-2944
nashville@sag-aftra.org

NEW ENGLAND
20 Park Plaza Suite 822
Boston, Massachusetts 02116
(617) 262-8001
newengland@sagaftra.org

OHIO-PITSBURGH
625 Stanwix St., Suite 2004
Pittsburgh, Pennsylvania 15222
(412) 281-6767

PHILADELPHIA
230 South Broad Street, Suite 500
Philadelphia, Pennsylvania 19102-1229
(215) 723-0507
philadelphia@sagaftra.org

SAN FRANCISCO – NORTHERN CALIFORNIA
350 Sansome Street, Suite 900
San Francisco, California 94104
(415) 391-7510
sf@sagaftra.org

SEATTLE
123 Boylston Avenue East, Suite A
Seattle, Washington 98102
(206) 282-2506
seattle@sagaftra.org

WASHINGTON – MID ATLANTIC
7735 Old Georgetown Road, Suite 950
Bethesda, Maryland 20814
(301) 657-2560

COMMERCIAL PRINT VS. HIGH FASHION MODELING

There's a big difference between a Commercial Print Model and a High Fashion Model. Modeling Agencies tend to have stricter requirements. For example, for a woman to become a High Fashion Model, she needs to be between 5'8"–5'11" in height and between the ages of 13–24. For men, you have to be 5'11"–6'3" and between the ages of 15–30.

However, if an agent is truly interested in your look, you do not have to meet all these requirements to get signed. High Fashion Modeling focuses more on Runway, Fashion, and, of course, Print Modeling. Commercial Print Modeling Agencies are a bit more open to signing talent that aren't necessarily a certain age or height. Keep in mind that if you are serious about taking the modeling route, your appearance is everything. You must stay fit and maintain your physique.

Today, Modeling Agencies have a Sports/Special Department. So, if you are great at a particular sport, you are in luck. Casting directors are sending out audition notices for commercials that involve different sports on a daily basis. If you possess high level skills in a specific sport, an agent can take interest in you and potentially sign you. Like Headshots, **Comp Cards** used to be very common for models to show at auditions. A Comp Card serves as the latest and best of a model's portfolio and is used as a business card. Like I mentioned before, your entire profile is now online. Casting directors aren't taking physical Headshots or Comp Cards these days, so I wouldn't worry too much about having them printed. In case of an emergency, you can always go to your local FedEx Office Print & Ship Center, Staples, or Office Depot and have your Comp Card/ Headshot printed.

In case you are wondering what Commercial Print is, it is modeling for covers and pages of publications advertising goods and services. When you go to the mall and see giant posters advertising a product, that's Commercial Print. Commercial Print auditions are different from regular Commercial auditions. You don't have to worry about memorizing lines or reading off a Cue card during a Print audition. They book you off your personality and look. Print auditions can sometimes take long, since they often have cattle calls—meaning you can tell a friend to come with you if they have the right fit for it. Once you are in the room, it's a fast process. You usually shoot several photos that vary from smiling to neutral looks, and sometimes even your hands, so be sure to keep your fingernails sharp. Some models even make a career from hand modeling. At the end of your audition, you might be asked a couple questions, which will showcase your personality, so always be sure to keep that good energy and smile big because looks can only take you so far.

The following is a list of some modeling agencies in Los Angeles as of 2019

ASTON MODELS
www.astonmodels.com

BELLA AGENCY
www.bellaagency.com

BMG MODELS & TALENT
www.bmgmodels.com

ENVY MODEL MANAGEMENT
www.envymodelmanagement.com

FORD MODELS
www.fordmodels.com

FREEDOM MODELS
www.freedommodels.com

IMG MODELS
www.imgmodels.com

LA MODELS
www.lamodels.com

MAVRICK MODELS
www.mavrickagency.com

MP MANAGEMENT
www.mpmanagement.com

NEWMARK MODELS
www.newmarkmodels.com

NEXT MODEL MANAGEMENT
www.nextmanagement.com

NOMAD MANAGEMENT
www.nomadmgmt.com

NTA MODEL MANAGEMENT
www.ntamodels.com

OTTO MODELS
www.ottomodels.com

PALOMA MODEL & TALENT
www.palomamodelandtalent.com

PEAK MODELS & TALENT
www.peakmodels.com

PHOTOGENICS
www.photogenicsmedia.com

STATE MANAGEMENT LOS ANGELES
www.statemgmt.com

THE FIRM LA MODEL & TALENT
www.firmlamodeltalent.com

THE LIONS
www.thelionsla.com

THE OSBRINK AGENCY
www.osbrinkagency.com

TWO MANAGEMENT
www.twomanagement.com

VISION
www.visionlosangeles.com

WILHELMINA MODELS
www.wilhelmina.com

AUDITIONS

When you get an audition notification through text or email, you can either Confirm, Reschedule, or Decline it. Never confirm an audition you can't make. If you confirm an audition and do not show up, you have wasted your time, the casting director's time, and most likely will not be called in for future projects. When you received your audition, it was because the casting director loved your look and picked you out of hundreds of actors. The casting director could have given your audition to another actor but decided to give it to you. Always be considerate, thankful, and professional if you want to maintain a great reputation here in Hollywood.

Be sure to give yourself extra time to get ready and arrive early to an audition. Being on time is not being on time. Showing up fifteen minutes earlier than your original call time says a lot about your character.

You may not believe it, but a lot of casting directors look at the sign-in sheets to check whether you were late or on time to your audition.

Dress the part for your audition. The more you look like the role you are going in for, the better your chances are of getting that callback—or even booking the job. Wearing costumes, accessories, and props to fit your role is always the way to go.

When going to a theatrical audition that requires a lot of dialogue, it's important to be off-book. Do your homework, study hard, and memorize your lines. When the day comes to audition, you'll be prepared, strong, and ready to Rock 'N' Roll. If you do not have time to memorize your lines for your audition, at least familiarize yourself with the script. It's perfectly fine to hold on to your script for backup during your audition. If at any point during your audition you get nervous or forget your lines, never stop—keep going and improvise. A lot of actors like to stick to the script, but improvisation is also good. Many casting directors enjoy watching actors improvise just to see something different, what you bring to the table. Never overdo it, though. Try to stay on book as much as possible.

Commercial auditions are a little easier, since the majority of them have **cue cards** inside the room, from which you will read. If you forget your dialogue, you can always peek at the cue card for backup. A cue card is also known as a note card. Cue cards are giant cards with words written on them. They are located right next to the camera to help actors remember what they have to say.

Your personality plays a big part in commercial auditions. Aside from memorizing your lines and being a natural great performer, your personality is very important. When you walk in that room, be sure to greet everyone, smile big, and bring that positive energy. Believe me, your audition starts the moment you walk in the room.

If I had a nickel for every time I absolutely killed an audition and did not get the part—well, you know. Rejection plays a big part in the life of an actor. Our profession deals with a lot of rejection and judgment from complete strangers, so you must mentally prepare yourself for that. You will deal with a lot of NOs, but that's just the game. It's not because you aren't good enough, so don't ever take it personally. What I've learned to do that has helped me throughout my career as an actor is to put the audition behind me as soon as I leave the room. I completely forget about it and move on. If I get the callback or book it, I get it. If I don't, then it wasn't for me. Try to set your mind on auditioning for as many projects as you can because eventually you will book a role, and it'll be the greatest feeling in the world.

Auditions can be very nerve-wracking. If you are a shy person or get nervous under pressure easily, I recommend you look into acting schools. Attending an acting school can help you boost your confidence and prepare you for future auditions. It's a process to book a project. Usually they have callbacks and narrow down the list to the actors they originally brought in. Getting a callback is a big deal, so if you get one you should feel very proud of yourself. A callback means the casting director and perhaps others involved liked what they saw in your first audition and decided to bring you in again for the project. You are one step closer to booking it.

Sometimes, when it's hard to choose the right actor for the role, they'll set up a third and final callback. Directors and producers sit in on final callbacks to watch you perform and meet you in person. Always remember that you are the star. It's your time in that room, and they are there to see you.

Casting directors meet and see plenty of actors on a regular basis. After coming in several times to read for a casting director, that director will begin to remember you. Always be professional and build a great relationship with a casting director because you never know what can happen down the line. I once auditioned to play a Host for an MTV show at Blanca Valdez Casting in West Hollywood, CA. I didn't get the part, but months later, I was on a set for another project when I received a phone call from Blanca Valdez. Blanca told me she had come across my MTV Host audition tape and was in need of a Host to guest star in Hulu's hit show *East Los High*. She then personally booked me on the show and brought me back the third season as the same character. Blanca remembered me and kept me in mind. You never know what can happen, so always be at your best behavior.

BACKGROUND WORK

Starting out your career as an actor can be tough in Los Angeles, especially if you are an independent person and have to pay your own bills. Waitressing, bartending, even driving Lyft are always great choices for work on the side. If you love being on-set, behind the scenes, and simply around acting, I encourage you to try Background Work. Any TV or movie extras you've ever seen on your favorite shows or movies are called Background Artists. You can earn a good living working background. I did Background Work for eleven years and learned a lot doing it. I always thought of Background Work as free acting school, since you get to work with your favorite actors, learn from them, and watch them perform live.

Background Work is also free film school in a way, since you get to be behind cameras a lot and learn what everyone's job is, from a Director to a Personal Assistant. Another reason you should consider doing Background Work is to get your three Union SAG-AFTRA vouchers. If you aren't SAG-AFTRA and start working Background, you will be working under blue Non-Union vouchers and getting paid minimum wage. Union Background Actors get yellow vouchers and a higher pay, since they've already joined SAG-AFTRA.

It's very difficult to get Union vouchers today but not impossible. Yellow Union vouchers aren't handed out easily. The last thing you want to do is ask for one on a set. It is very unprofessional to do so and may result in you never getting called back to work again. My advice is to always be extremely professional on a set. Show up early and be respectful to the person checking you in. Sometimes a Union person scheduled to work for the day may cancel due to an emergency, so they'll have an extra Union voucher sitting around. So, always try to be on your best behavior.

There are several Background Casting Companies you can register with here in Los Angeles. The biggest ones I recommend are Central Casting, Bill Dance Casting, Rich King Casting, and Jeff Olan Casting. If you are the right fit for a featured background role on a television show or feature film, the casting directors at these agencies have the power to book you under a Union voucher. If you get the opportunity to register with these or any other Background Agencies, never turn down their work and always be on your best behavior with them.

When I was in my early twenties, I got booked to work on Disney Channel's *A.N.T. Farm* as a background performer. During work, I was randomly selected to play the school mascot, Wacky the Wolf. They then used me in a scene, which turned out to be hilarious, and they decided to write Wacky the Wolf's character into most of the episodes. I got upgraded to a Principal Performer, and my rate went up. The chances of getting upgraded working background to a Principal Performer on a television show or feature film are very small. Production avoids this as much as possible since they are on a budget and it will cost them more money. However, it *can* happen to you, if you are in the right place at the right time.

Working Background in commercials is great money. You can make over $200 a day if you are Non-Union and over $350 a day if you are SAG-AFTRA. The chances of getting upgraded to a Principal Performer working Background on a commercial are very good. Commercials do not work like television or feature films. In television and feature films, they can heavily feature you as long as you don't have any speaking lines, and you'll still be considered a Background Performer and get paid the Background rate. In the commercial world, it's quite the opposite. If you get heavily featured and are visibly seen working Background on a commercial, you'll get upgraded to a Principal Performer. If you are Non-Union, you'll get an additional check mailed out to you and can make a few hundred dollars more. If you are Union, however, you'll get the Principal Upgrade contract sent for you to fill out, and you can make thousands of dollars down the line in residuals.

The following is a list of Background Casting Companies and Commercial Background Agencies with which you can register in Los Angeles as of 2019

BACKGROUND CASTING COMPANIES

BILL DANCE CASTING
4605 Lankershim Blvd. Suite 219
North Hollywood, CA 91602
(818) 754-6634
www.billdancecasting.com

CENTRAL CASTING
220 S. Flower St, Burbank, CA 91502
(818) 562-2700
www.centralcasting.com

JEFF OLAN CASTING
14044 Ventura Blvd, Suite 209
Sherman Oaks, CA 91423
(818) 377-4475
www.jeffolancasting.com

RICH KING CASTING
6671 Sunset Blvd #1585 Room 101
Los Angeles, CA 90028
(323) 993-01100
info@richkingcasting.net
www.richkingcasting.net

COMMERCIAL BACKGROUND AGENCIES

ADVANCED CASTING & TALENT
actextras@gmail.com
www.actextras.com

ALICE ELLIS CASTING
submissions@elliscasting.com
www.elliscasting.com

COMMERCIAL EXTRAS
register.commercialextras@gmail.com
www.commercial-extras.com

EXTRA EXTRA CASTING
submissions@extraextracasting.com
www.extraextracasting.com

EXTRAS ON AVAIL CASTING
registration@extrasonavail.com
www.extrasonavail.com

IDELL JAMES CASTING
ijcphoto@me.com
www.idelljames.com

PEAS & CARROTS CASTING
talent@peasandcarrots.com
www.peasandcarrotscasting.com

PRIME CASTING
info@primecasting.com
www.primecasting.com

CALLING SERVICES

If you are looking to do Background Work for income, I highly encourage you to register with a Calling Service. A Calling Service is a Talent Listing service that helps Background Actors find work in television, films, and commercials. To register with a Calling Service, you must reach out to them through email and hope to hear back. You can also attempt to contact their office number by phone, but before doing so, I suggest you visit their website first. Casting Companies like Central Casting, Bill Dance Casting, and

Rich King Casting all work with Calling Services to hire Background Actors for work. It's an easier process to book Talent from Calling Services, since they can physically go on their website's database and check out Background Actors Profiles.

Calling Services can charge you a monthly fee, which ranges from $60–$85 a month, or they can charge you a smaller percentage per booking. Once you are registered with a Calling Service, you will have access to your own profile on their database, where you can list yourself available or unavailable Monday–Sunday. Some Calling Services even allow you to upload your headshots, vehicle, personal information, skills, and sizes. Once you are registered with a Calling Service, it's imperative that you understand you do not ask them for Union vouchers. Calling Services have zero power towards that. In fact, it's casting directors who have that power, so always be on your best behavior with them.

It is the task of the Calling Service to send out your profile to casting directors and try to get you on a job. Some Calling Services are also able to book you on Print Jobs, Live Events, and in Featured Roles.

The following is a list of Calling Services with which you can register in Los Angeles as of 2019

BACKGROUND TALENT SERVICES
4804 Laurel Canyon Blvd, #739
North Hollywood, CA 91607
(818) 771-5727
www.backgroundtalent.net

BOOKED TALENT
7424 ½ Sunset Blvd, Suite #3
Los Angeles, CA 90046
(323) 883-1999
bookedtaelntdetails@gmail.com
www.bookedtalent.com

EXTRAS MANAGEMENT
207 S Flower St
Burbank, CA 91502
(818) 972-9474
kevin@extrasmngt.com
www.extrasmanagement.com

FACE2FACE MANAGEMENT
3727 W Magnolia Blvd #414
Burbank, CA 91505
(818) 748-1550
submissions@face2facela.com
www.face2facela.com

JESSICA'S A LIST
1920 Hillhurst Ave
Los Angeles, CA 90027
(323) 661-6064
submit@jessicasalist.com
www.jessicasalist.com

JOEYS LIST
info@joeyslist.com
www.joeyslist.com

UNCUT CASTING SERVICES
3877 Grand View Blvd Suite B
Los Angeles, CA 90066
info@uncutcasting.com
www.launcutcasting.com

STANDING-IN

Standing-in can always be a good choice for work. It's fun, easy, and if you become a regular Stand-in on a television show or feature film, you might even get invited to the wrap party when they are done filming. A Stand-in on a set fills in for the Principal Actor when he or she is not being used for rehearsals, camera blocking, and lighting setups. When the cinematographers have covered all angles and are good and ready to film, the Stand-ins step out and Principal Actors step in to film. Casting directors always aim to hire experienced Stand-ins, but usually the main reason a Stand-in would get hired is because he or she fits the Principal Actor's height, build, hair color, and skin complexion. It isn't always like this, but casting directors typically try to match the Principal Actor's look as much as possible to cover their shots perfectly.

I remember Standing-in for Carlos PenaVega from *Big Time Rush* on a Nintendo commercial years ago, and the entire crew telling me how identical we were in height, weight, and size. We even had a similar haircut, so I knew right away why I had been booked to be his Stand-in. In many cases, directors ask Stand-ins to read off the scripts and act out the scenes for them. You must be prepared to do that. Stand-in Performers get paid a higher rate than Background Performers. If you ever get booked to be a Stand-in on a television show or feature film, I encourage you to do your best on set. Production will ask casting directors to check your availability to come back to set and work for them again. You can then potentially become a Regular Stand-in and make a lot of money, depending on how long they are filming.

When you become a Regular Stand-in on a television show or feature film, and remain doing a great job, production can be more flexible with your schedule. If you ever have an important audition or need to call in sick due to an emergency, production will most likely be cool with it. My buddy, Mike, was Aziz Ansari's Regular Stand-in on the show *Parks and Recreation,* and when he couldn't come in to work due to an emergency, he'd have me cover for him. Of course, he'd always check with production first and get approval, and they then reached out to the casting directors at central casting to book me on the show.

There's been cases where a Regular Stand-in was so great at his or her job that, in the case of an emergency where production needed an actor for a specific shot that got added for the day, the director gave the role to the Stand-in as a thank you. If that ever happened to any Stand-in, production is forced to bring out a Principal Performer Contract for the Stand-in to fill out. The Stand-in then gets upgraded to a Principal Performer for the day, and they make a lot of money in residuals down the line—if the project is SAG-AFTRA.

PHOTO-DOUBLING

Many times during filming, production companies may not get to shoot specific shots with their Principal Actors due to time and schedule. If a production can get away with filming the shots they need without physically having to bring back their Principal Performers to set, they'd much rather hire Photo Doubles to do the job. Bringing back their Principal Actors days, weeks, or months after filming to cover those shots can cost a lot of money, so production companies avoid this as much as possible. Photo Doubles must resemble actors as closely as possible in height, build, hair color, and skin complexion.

When you are hired as a Photo Double on a set, wardrobe will dress you in the same clothes the Principal Performer is wearing to match them in the scene. Often Photo Doubles are asked if they are willing to Body Double the Principal Actor in a nude scene—of course, for a higher rate. Photo Doubles are also used to do inserts, such as picking up an object, placing an object down, or even shaking a hand. Usually when Photo Doubles are hired for inserts, they'll be on a set for a few hours.

I had a great time doing inserts for Wilmer Valderrama on the show *NCIS*. I worked the show multiple times Photo Doubling Wilmer, since he was filming those days and couldn't do the scenes himself. Those were some of my favorite times being on set, since the crew was very welcoming, professional, and kind.

If you are a Stunt Performer, you can make a lot of money Photo-Doubling Principal Actors. The majority of time, actors cannot perform special skills or their own stunts, so production hires a Stunt Performer to Photo Double them. If you Photo Double an actor and do stunts for them, you'll get the stunt performer contract and get paid a lot for the day. You will also make residuals down the line if the project is SAG-AFTRA. If you just Photo Double, Body Double, Hand Double, or do Inserts for the day, your rate will be similar to a Stand-in's rate.

STUNTS

Stunts can be very dangerous and require tremendous focus, training, preparation, discipline, performance abilities, and precise skills, which is why production companies would much rather hire experienced Stunt Performers to be safe instead of using Principal Actors. A lot of actors enjoy doing their own stunts, but production companies avoid this as much as possible so as not to risk their actors getting injured. If an actor injured him or herself on a set, it would be a disaster. This happening would cost a production a lot of money, since they'd have to wait for the actor to completely heal to start filming again, which could take days, weeks, or months.

Remember Brad Pitt hurting himself very badly while filming 2004's *Troy*? Pitt tore his left Achilles tendon while filming a fight scene on set and delayed production for several months. Tom Cruise also broke his ankle doing his own stunt in *Mission Impossible Fallout,* and Daniel Craig had his right shoulder reconstructed, left and right knee operated on, and even lost his two front teeth filming his James Bond films.

If you are looking to start a career in Stunts, I encourage you to start working on building your Stunt Reel. A Stunt Reel is a video stunt performers use to showcase their work to stunt coordinators and producers who may be looking to hire them. Stunt coordinators and casting directors want to know that they can trust you to perform on set, so they'll always ask to see your Stunt Reel.

Stunt work is a very close-knit community and can be extremely difficult to join if you do not know a professional

stunt performer or stunt coordinator. Attending professional Stunt Academies and joining professional Stunt Directories are some other ways to begin professional work. As a stunt performer, you can get paid very comfortably for the day, usually hundreds of dollars. If you get hired to do stunts on a Union television show or feature film, you can make residuals down the line for your work day. There is plenty of work for stunt performers in television, feature films, commercials, and even music videos. The more special skills you acquire, the more you'll work in town. Fighting and weaponry skills are very common in the stunt world. If you are a military veteran or know mixed martial arts, that can be a very great deal for you. Being highly skilled in a specific sport can also benefit you in the stunt world.

If you are SAG-AFTRA or eligible, I recommend you go on Facebook and look up JMP Productions, INC.-Talent page. It's a private group that specializes in stunts. Their goal is to help Talent find more jobs and help coordinators find new Talent. No negativity is allowed on their page.

DIVERSITY IN HOLLYWOOD

Hollywood has changed throughout the years. Nowadays, anyone can become an actor providing they have the right attitude, ambition, and determination. You don't need to have chiseled abs or look like a model to be successful in Hollywood. Of course, taking care of yourself physically and caring about your health and appearance is very important, but having a relatable look, looking ethnically ambiguous, or even being from the LGBTQ community is much more accepted these days. There's a lot of castings for interracial and same sex couples today, which you did not see much before. We didn't have

African American cast superhero films like *Black Panther*, which grossed over $1 Billion in earnings, or an all Asian cast American film like *Crazy Rich Asians*, which crushed box offices and became the highest-grossing romantic comedy of the last ten years.

Films with female leads kicking ass, such as *Captain Marvel* and *Wonder Woman*, did not exist back in the day. Hollywood is more representative of diversity and inclusion today, and this is shown by American shows like FX's *Mayans M.C.*, or *Vida* on Starz. Netflix has also played a huge factor in opening doors to minority actors and giving them opportunities to lead in big feature films and TV shows, which aren't so stereotypical.

If you are looking to begin a career in acting, there is no better time to start. There is plenty of work for anyone willing to work hard and push themselves to succeed in this business. We are living in the future, and we have come a long way in terms of equality. There is still work to be done, but it is getting better. Hollywood has Revolutionized throughout the years, and we are living in the new era.

FILM SET TERMS

1ˢᵗ Team, Talent, or Heroes: Principal Actors or Models

2ⁿᵈ Team: Stand-ins

First A D: Assistant Director

Second A D: Second Assistant Director

Crew: Production Staff On Set

Crew Call: Time shooting is scheduled to begin for the day

Green Room: Area given to Talent to rest

Background Holding: Area given to Background actors to rest

Craft Services: Food, Drinks, and Snacks provided for Talent, Background, and Crew

Picture's Up: They are about to roll and shoot a take

Quiet On Set: No talking, No cell phones, and No walking around

Speed: Camera is rolling

Mark: A mark on the floor with gaffer tape, which tells the actor where he or she needs to land in order to be in focus for the camera

Closed Set: You are not allowed on a closed set unless you are Talent or Crew

First Positions: Go back to the start of the scene

Last Positions: Go back to your last positions from your last scene

Cheat: To falsify the actor's original first position to best suit the camera

Cut: End of take

New Deal: Moving on to a new camera setup

Magic Hour: When the light changes from daylight to dusk

Meal Penalty: They don't break you in time for lunch, so Production has to pay you more money

B-Roll: To add detail, cutaways, or emotion to the scene

ADR: Automated Dialogue Replacement

MOS (Mit Out Sound): Filming without sound being recorded

POV: Point of View

Martini Shot: The very last shot in Production for the day

Wrap: Done filming for the day

MODELS IN PHOTOS

NEW TO LA
New City Girl: Monica Marquez
Photographer: Luis Blanco

Los Angeles
Photographer: Raul A Flores

GETTING AN AGENT
Agent: Christian Campos
Actor: Adam Aguilar
Photographer: Adam Aguilar

ACTORS WEBSITES
Nurse: Hilsin Garcia
Soccer Player: Garrett Plotkin
Photographer: Garrett Plotkin

Couple: Christian Campos and Veronica Lopez
Photographer: Jamaal Murray

INVESTING IN YOUR CAREER
Commercial Headshot: Veronica Lopez
Theatrical Headshot: Christian Campos
Photographer: Jamaal Murray

Ring Light Woman: Veronica Lopez
Photographer: Adam Aguilar

COMMERCIAL PRINT MODELING VS.
HIGH FASHION MODELING
Shirtless Model: Indar Smith
Photographer: Luke Fontana

Jean Jacket Model: Evan Gomez
Photographer: Adam Brown

High Fashion Model: Nicko Sabado
Photographer: Sam Pick

AUDITIONS
Actor: Christian Campos

CALLING SERVICES
Woman on Couch: Veronica Lopez
Photographer: Adam Aguilar

STANDING-IN
Stand-In: Christian Campos
Photographer: Adam Aguilar

STUNTS
Motorcycle Rider: Jake Pierce Ryan
Photographer: Marc Pineda

Skateboarder: Garrett Plotkin
Photographer: Garrett Plotkin

Navy Seal: Stephan Perez

DIVERSITY IN HOLLYWOOD
Group of Friends: Christian Campos, Gareth Phillips, Nicko Sabado, Myke Wilken, Troy Hatt

Interracial Couple: Orel De La Mota, Brooke Morrison

Same-Sex Couple Men: Aaron Drake, Jake Drake

PHOTOGRAPHERS' INFORMATION

Adam Aguilar
www.AguilarAdam.com
adam@aguilaradam.com
Instagram: AguilarAdam

Adam Brown
adambrown@yahoo.com
Instagram: ThatGuyAdamB

Jamaal Murray
www.photosbyjamaal.com
contact@photosbyjamaal.com
Instagram: PhotosbyJamaal

Luke Fontana
www.LukeFontana.com
lukefontanaphoto@gmail.com
Instagram: LukeFontana

Raul A Flores
Raulflore7@gmail.com
Instagram: polo_photoart

Sam Pick
sampick19@gmail.com
Instagram: SDRPICK

ACKNOWLEDGEMENTS

LOVE, RESPECT, AND HONOR: To my parents, Mario and Silvia Campos, for raising me, giving me endless love, guidance, support, and most importantly, giving me the opportunity to have been born a first-generation American citizen. To my older brother, Pierre Campos, for always protecting me and being my first role model. To my grandmother, Matilde Escobar, for always being there all my life, cooking for me and giving me unconditional love. To my aunts, uncles, cousins, and all my beautiful nieces and nephews, I hope I've made you proud. To my best friends, whom I consider brothers, Gerard Martinez, Pedro Medina, Juan Morales, Garrett Plotkin, Nicko Sabado, Fredy Alberto, Huy Bui, Manuel Rodriguez, Marcus Grimaldo, Jose Rivera, Ahmadreza Parayandeh, and Eric Arroyo, I love you guys.

MY MENTORS: Ben W. Decker, I came to you with this dream of mine asking for guidance. I wanted to make a difference in the world by writing this book for new actors who wanted to chase their dream but did not know where to start. You took me under your wing, believed in me, and showed me the way. I love you, brother.

BOBBY GENE, you gave me a career and more importantly, an opportunity to do something I love. I'll forever be appreciative for what you did. Thank you for giving me my first audition, thank you for showing me the ropes, and thank you for being a great friend.

GARRETT PLOTKIN, you've always been there to hear me out. You've given me the best advice without ever judging me. You seize the day as if it were your last and live life to the fullest. I've never heard you talk about anyone else in a negative way. Thank you for inspiring me every day.

HUY BUI, we met in Long Beach years ago, and you've gone above and beyond to celebrate my birthdays, welcome me to your homes, and given me life advice for a better future. You are one of the realist people I've ever met. I know you are a very private person, so thank you for being an older brother to me.

VERONICA LOPEZ, I've learned a lot from you through these years. You've taught me how to love more and to appreciate today and the things I have in front of me because they may not be here tomorrow. You are the kindest person and possess the biggest, most caring heart in the world. You've been my biggest support throughout this journey, so thank you.

MARCUS GRIMALDO, we've been through some good and rough times together, and I've seen you accomplish so much in your career. I'm extremely proud of you and so grateful to have you by my side to support me no matter what. Thanks for being my older brother.

SEAN MCCLAM, thank you so much for going out of your way and doing so much for me. You were the first person I reached out to for advice, and you've been there for me to this day. You are a great friend and mentor. Your actions do not go unnoticed, so thank you.

DWAYNE JOHNSON, you truly are changing the world with your words and kindness. Listening to you inspires me to never give up on my dreams and to push myself to my fullest potential. Your words give me life, brother, so thank you for always putting your fans first.

LEONARDO DICAPRIO, you are my favorite actor and the perfect example of giving back. Thank you for caring about our world and for being the best environmentalist. Thank you for sharing your gift.

JOE ROGAN, your podcasts give me life. I truly learn a lot from you every day. Your videos are so educational and my favorites to watch. You touch on every topic. You are an amazing human being. Never change.

MY FRIENDS: There are too many of you to list, but I'm so thankful for all of you. If you are reading this, I want you to know that I love you very much and can't express enough how much joy I feel with the love and support you've given me. Whether you call to say hi, invite me to events, or follow me on social media and stay in touch. I appreciate all of you tremendously. I hope you are proud to call me your friend. I'll always be here if you need me. Love to all of you.

A SPECIAL THANKS: To all my wonderful friends, actors, models, and photographers for allowing me to use their photographs in my book.

REST IN PEACE: To my grandfather, Roberto Arevalo Gordillo, whom I miss every day and wish I would have had the honor of meeting. To my dear friend, Jesus "Bucky" Martinez, I dedicate this accomplishment to you. We grew up and always talked about our goals and dreams. I miss you every day. To Virginia Esparza who I'll always love like a mother, thank you for always welcoming me with open arms, and always calling me your adopted son. I love you all so much and will always hold you close to my heart.

ABOUT THE AUTHOR

CHRISTIAN A. CAMPOS is an American actor and model born and raised in Los Angeles, California. After completing High School, Christian attended the Los Angeles Film School in Hollywood and graduated with a degree in directing and editing. Since then, he has guest-starred in popular TV shows, such as *Criminal Minds*, *NCIS*, and *East Los High*, and he continues to appear in various commercials for worldwide companies like Pepsi, AT&T, Best Buy, and Adidas.

CPSIA information can be obtained
at www.ICGtesting.com
Printed in the USA
LVHW080405011019
632710LV00006B/368/P